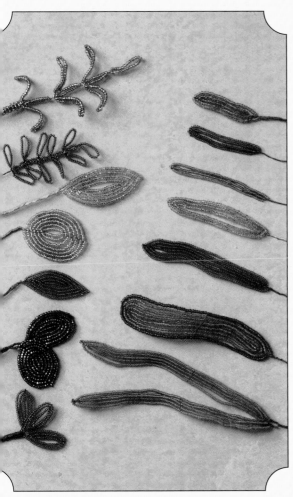

Single Loop Method

1. Cut the wire 5" - 6" longer than the finished height of the petal or leaf. Thread enough beads on the center of the wire to equal twice the height. Bend the wire in half.

2. Twist the ends of the wire below the loop to close the petal.

Single Loop Variations -

3. Make a Single Loop, then thread beads onto the ends of the wire.
4. Twist the wire below the beads and make a ingle Loop on each end of the ire. Bend the loops down at each side. Repeat.

, Or, twist the beads and make a Single Loop on ach end of the wire. Repeat.

Basic Techniques
Examples of leaf and petal shapes

Double Loop Method

1. Make a Single Loop as large as instructed.
2. Bead the end of one wire and make another Single Loop over the center of the first one. Twist the wires as before.

Center Bar Method

1. Thread enough beads on one wire to equal the length of the Center Bar as instructed. Bend over the top of the wire. Twist another wire with the center wire below the beads.
2. Thread beads onto the second wire. Wrap the top around the Center Bar.

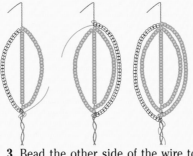

3. Bead the other side of the wire to form a **LOOP**. Wrap the wire and the bottom and repeat to make as many loops as called for in the instructions.

Bracing

Bracing is used to support long leaves and to shape some flowers.

Loop a piece of wire around each beaded wire cross the width of the piece

---

Loop according to the instructions.
2. Make another **Single Loop** on the end of one wire.

3. Continuous Petals are used to form **LAYERS**. Continue to make as many loops as required for the flower. Bend the loops around to form a 1/4" circle in the center. Twist the wires together to make a stem. Bend the stem down.

Levels

Make individual petals as instructed for the flower and wrap another wire around the stems to make one level of the flower.

Optional Stems

For larger or heavier flowers, bend a piece of floral wire over the stems of the petals. Wrap wire around the stems and the floral wire.

Calyx

Some stems have a calyx or hip.

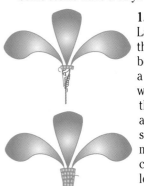

1. Form a Layer and thread seed beads onto another wire. Wrap the beads around the stems to make a calyx as long as instructed. Pull the end of the wire back up under the seed beads. Clip the wire end.

Orange Tiger Lily

Materials:
Garnet opaque, Green crystal, Yellow cryst[al] and Orange crystal seed beads; 28 gaug[e] wire; wire cutters; floral tape.

Stamen

Make 3 for each flower. Use Garne[t] beads to make a $1/2$" **Double Loo[p]** at one end of a wire. Twist the wi[re] twice around itself at the bottom [of] the loop. Clip the wire end. Threa[d] $1^1/2$" of Green beads on the oth[er] wire end. Twist the ends of the st[a]mens together.

Petal

Make 6 for each flower. Make a $3/[?]$ x 2" **Center Bar** petal with 3 loop[s] using a mixture of Yellow an[d] Orange beads. The center bar [is] $1^1/4$" long.

Leaf

Make 1 or 2 for each flower. Use Green beads to make a 2" **Double Loop**.

Assembly:

Arrange the petals around the stamen and floral tape the stems for 2". Add a leaf and tape for 2" more. Add optional second leaf on the other side of the stem.

White Day Lily

The message of a White lily is youthful innocence.

Materials:
Green crystal, Amber crystal and White-lined crystal seed beads; 28 gauge wire; wire cutters; floral tape.

Instructions:
Follow the instructions for the Tiger Lily to make the Day Lily.

Stamen - Use Amber and Green beads.
Petals - Use White-lined crystal beads.
Leaves - Use Green crystal beads.

ILLUSTRATIONS ARE SHOWN ACTUAL SIZE - REFER TO THE BASIC TECHNIQUES ON PAGE 2.

Chrysanthemum

A fall bloomer, a mum indicates hope in dark times.

Materials:
Yellow crystal and Green crystal seed beads; 28 gauge wire; 15" piece of floral wire; wire cutters; floral tape.

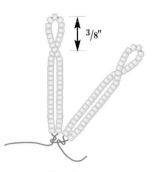

Top Layer
Make 9 continuous $1^1/_4$" **Single Loops**. Twist the loops $3/_8$" below the top.

Second Layer
Make 12 continuous $1^1/_2$" **Single Loops**.

Third Layer
Make 14 continuous $1^7/_8$" **Single Loops**.

Fourth Layer
Make 16 continuous $2^1/_4$" **Single Loops**.

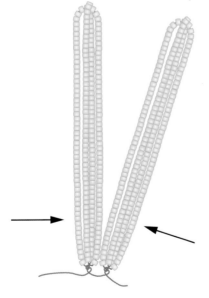

Fifth Layer
Make 20 continuous $2^3/_4$" **Single Loops**.

Bottom Layer
Make 20 continuous $2^3/_4$" **Double Loops**. Brace the loops together $1/_2$" above the bottom of the layer.

Calyx
Use the **Center Bar** technique to make a $1^1/_4$" circle with $5^1/_2$ loops. The center bar is $1/_2$" long. Bend the **Center Bar** into a semicircle and continue according to the Basic Technique on page 2. Pull the wire ends from the back up through the center circle. Tape these wire ends to the floral wire along with the layer stems.

Assembly:
Push the stem of each layer through the circles of the subsequent layers. Push the floral wire up through the layers to extend 1". Floral tape the layer wires in place to the floral wire. Bend all the loops upward and curve them slightly toward the center.

ILLUSTRATIONS ARE SHOWN ACTUAL SIZE - REFER TO THE BASIC TECHNIQUES ON PAGE 2.

Windflower

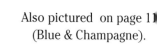

Also pictured on page 11
(Blue & Champagne).

Materials:
Black opaque or Champagne crystal, Bronze crystal, Silver-lined crystal or Blue-lined crystal and Green iridescent seed beads; 28 gauge wire; wire cutters; floral tape.

Stamen
Use Black beads (for Bronze flowers) or Champagne beads (for Silver and Blue flowers) to make a 1/4" x 3/8" **Center Bar** with 1 loop. The center bar is 1/4" long. Leave the wires 2" - 3" long.

Petal
Use Bronze, Silver or Blue beads to make 9 continuous 1/4" x 1" **Center Bar** petals with 1 loop. The center bar is 7/8" long. Leave the top of the **Center Bar** wire 25" long.

When the petal is finished, pull the center wire down behind the petal and wrap it around the wires at the bottom. Use the end of the **Center Bar** wire for the next petal. Repeat.

Leaf
(Pictured on page 2.)
Make as many as required for your arrangement. Use Green beads to make a 3 1/4" **Loop Tree** with 1" loops. Bend the loops down at each side. Make a 1/2" Calyx.

Assembly:
Lay the stamen across the center of the petal circle. Bend the wires over opposite sides of the circle and twist the ends together at the back.

ILLUSTRATIONS ARE SHOWN ACTUAL SIZE - REFER TO THE BASIC TECHNIQUES ON PAGE 2.

Tea Rose

Materials:
Coast crystal and Iridescent Gunmetal seed beads; 28 gauge wire; wire cutters; floral tape.

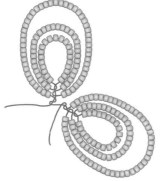

Top Layer
Make 4 continuous ¹/₂" **Single Loops**.

Second Layer
Make 3 continuous 1" petals with 3 graduating **Single Loops**.

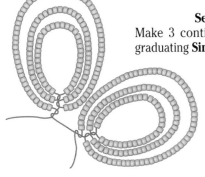

Bottom Layer
Make 5 continuous 1¹/₄" petals with 3 graduating **Single Loops**.

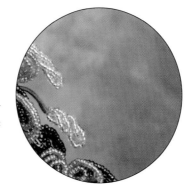

Leaf
Make 2 or 3 for each flower. Use Gunmetal beads to make a 1¹/₄" **Center Bar** with 4 loops. The center bar is ³/₈" long.

Assembly:
Push the stem of each layer through the circles of the subsequent layers. Arrange the leaves around the back of the flower. Floral tape all the stems together.

Petal Flowers

Materials:
Complementary color seed beads to match the flowers in any arrangement and Green crystal seed beads (optional); 28 gauge wire; wire cutters; floral tape.

Make a 1¹/₂" **Single Loop**. Twist the top half once. Twist the bottom half once. Fold the top down and thread one of the bottom wires through the top loop. Twist the bottom wires together to form the stem. Twist the bud again.

NOTE: Buds may be added as filler stems to an arrangement or they may be taped onto a stem below a flower.

**Leaves
(Optional)**
Use Green beads to make 2 continuous ⁷/₈" **Single Loops**. Twist the wires together. Tape the stems of the buds and the leaves together. Cup the leaves up to cradle the buds.

ILLUSTRATIONS ARE SHOWN ACTUAL SIZE - REFER TO THE BASIC TECHNIQUES ON PAGE 2.

Rose

Red and Orange roses indicate deep and passionate love.

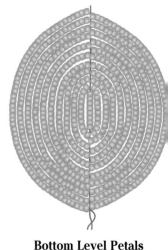

Materials:
Seed Beads - Dark Orange/Red crystal and Dark Green crystal; 28 gauge wire; wire cutters; floral tape; floral wire.

Center Petals
Make 2 each for the rose and the bud. Use the Orange/Red beads to make a 1" **Center Bar** with 5 loops. The center bar is $1/4$" long.

Second Level Petals
Make 2 each for the rose and the bud. Use the Orange/Red beads to make a $1 1/4$" **Center Bar** with 7 loops. The center bar is $1/4$" long.

Third Level Petals
Make 4 for the rose. Use the Orange/Red beads to make a $1 3/4$" **Center Bar** with 7 loops. The center bar is $3/8$" long.

Bottom Level Petals
Make 6 for the rose. Use the Orange/Red beads to make a 2 **Center Bar** with 10 loops. The center bar is $1/2$" long.

Flower Leaves
Make 5 for the rose, make 4 for the bud. Use Dark Green beads to make a 1" **Center Bar** with 2 loops. The center bar is $1/2$" long.

Stem Leaves
Make 3 for each rose and bud stem. Use Dark Green beads to make a $1 1/2$" **Center Bar** with 6 loops. The center bar is $3/8$" long.

Assembly:
Bend the edges of each petal up to form cupped shapes. Overlap the petals of each level. Arrange the leaves around the back of the flower. Floral tape all the stems together. Wrap the stems of the Stem Leaves individually.

ILLUSTRATIONS ARE SHOWN ACTUAL SIZE - REFER TO THE BASIC TECHNIQUES ON PAGE 2.

Allium

An allium speaks of good fortune and prosperity.

Materials:
Rose crystal, Purple crystal, Pink crystal, Toast crystal, Yellow-lined crystal and Green crystal seed beads; 28 gauge wire; wire cutters; floral tape.

Stamen

Use Yellow beads (for Rose or Pink flowers), Toast beads (for Purple flowers) or Purple beads (for Toast Flowers) to make 4 continuous $3/8$" **Single Loops**.

Top Layer
Make 8 continuous $3/8$" **Single Loops**. Overlap edges of the petals slightly.

Second Layer
Make 12 continuous $3/8$" **Single Loops**. Overlap edges of the petals a bit more.

Third Layer
Make 15 continuous $3/8$" **Single Loops**. Overlap edges of the petals a bit more.

Fourth Layer

Make 18 continuous $3/8$" **Single Loops**. Overlap the edges of the petals halfway, so the petals are stacked side by side.

Flower Leaves
Use Green beads to make 7 continuous $1/2$" **Single Loops**. Overlap the edges and bend the leaves downward a bit.

Stem Leaves

Make 1 or 2 for each stem. Use Green beads to make a 2" **Center Bar** with 6 loops. The center bar is $1/2$" long.

Floweret

Flowerets
Make 1 for each stem to match the flower. Make 3 continuous **Single Loops**. Begin with a $3/4$" loop, then make one $1/2$" loop, followed by another $3/4$" loop. Pull the loops to form a stack and twist. Twist the ends of the wires together.

Floweret Leaves
Use Green beads to make 1 for each floweret. Make 4 continuous **Single Loops**. Alternate two $5/8$" loops with two $7/8$" loops. Pull the loops to cradle the floweret with the shorter leaves at the sides.

Assembly:
Push the stem of each layer through the circles of the subsequent layers. Tape all the stems together for $1 3/4$", then add a floweret. Tape the stems for 1" and add a stem leaf or two to the stem. Complete taping the stem until it is the desired length, adding a length of floral wire as needed.

ILLUSTRATIONS ARE SHOWN ACTUAL SIZE - REFER TO THE BASIC TECHNIQUES ON PAGE 2.

Gardenia

Materials:
White-lined crystal and Green crystal seed beads; 28 gauge wire; wire cutters; floral tape; floral wire.

Center Petals
Use White beads to make 4 continuous ¹/₄" **Single Loops**.

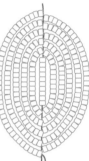

Second Level
Make 4. Use White bead to make a 1" **Center Ba** with 3 loops. The Cente Bar is ¹/₄" long.

Third Level
Make 6. Use White beads to make a 1¹/₄" **Center Bar** with 4 loops. The center bar is ³/₈" long.

Fourth Level
Make 8. U White beads make a 1¹/ **Center B** with loops. Th center b is ¹/₂" long

Gardenia Assembly:
Arrange each level. Wrap the stems for ³/₄". Push the calyx u the stem and bend the leaves up to cup the bottom of th flower. Floral tape the stems together, adding the small leave then the large leaves, 1" apart on opposite sides of the stem

Yellow Freesia

Send freesias as a sign that love can be careful and calm.

Materials:
Yellow crystal and Green crystal seed beads; 28 gauge wire; wire cutters; floral tape; floral wire.

Center Petals
Make 2 for each the freesia and the bud. Use Yellow beads to make 1" **Center Bars** with 4 loops. The center bar is ¹/₄" long.

Second Level
Make 3 for each the freesia and the bud. Use Yellow beads to make a 1¹/₄" **Center Bar** with 5 loops. The center bar is ¹/₄" long.

Third Level
Make 6 for the freesia. U Yellow beads to make a 1¹/ **Center Bar** with 7 loop The center bar is ¹/₄" long.

Stem Leaves
Make 3 for separate stems behind the freesia and the bud. Use Green beads to make a 1³/₈" **Center Bar** with 5 loops. The center bar is ³/₈" long.

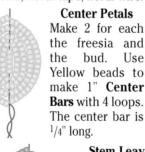

Assembly:
Bend the edges of each petal up up slightly. Bend bac the tops of the outer 2 levels. Overlap the petals of eac level. Arrange the small leaves around the back of th flowers. Floral tape all the stems together. Wrap th stems of the Stem Leaves individually.

Flower Leaves
Make 5 for the freesia, make 4 for the bud. Use Green beads to make a 1" **Center Bar** with 2 loops. The center bar is ¹/₂" long.

ILLUSTRATIONS ARE SHOWN ACTUAL SIZE - REFER TO THE BASIC TECHNIQUES ON PAGE 2.

Gardenias mean grace.

Calyx
Make 1 for each flower. Use Green beads to make 12 continuous 1" **Single Loops**.

Small Stem Leaves (Gardenia)
Make 4 for each stem. Use Green beads to make a $1^1/2$" **Center Bar** with 3 loops. The center bar is $3/8$" long.

Large Stem Leaves (Gardenia)
Make 4 for each stem. Use Green beads to make a $1^3/4$" **Center Bar** with 4 loops. The center bar is $1/2$" long.

Clematis

Materials:
White-lined crystal, Green crystal and Red opaque seed beads; 28 gauge wire; wire cutters; floral tape; floral wire.

Petals
Use the White beads to make 5 continuous $5/8$" **Double Loops**. Twist the wire ends once. Thread 2 Red beads onto one wire end. Bend the beaded wire across the center of the flower and over the circle to the back. Bend the unbeaded wire to the back. Twist the wires together below the center circle.

Assembly:
Make 3 flowers. Bead the stems of each flower with Green beads for 2". Lay the ends of the stems along a length of floral wire, wrap with tape.

Anemone

Anemones speak of abandonment.

Materials:
Pink-lined crystal and Yellow crystal seed beads; 28 gauge wire; wire cutters; floral tape.

Stamen
Use the Yellow beads to make 4 continuous $1/8$" **Single Loops**.

Large Flower
Make 4 petals for each flower. Use the Pink beads to make $3/4$" **Center Bar** petals with $3^1/2$ loops The center bar is $1/4$" long.

Small Flower
Make 4 petals for each flower. Use the Pink beads to make $1/2$" **Center Bar** petals with $2^1/2$ loops The center bar is $1/4$" long.

Assembly:
Make 2 large flowers and 1 small flower for each stem. Wrap the stem of one large flower for $1^1/2$". Wrap each of the other flower stems for 1". Add the other large flower, wrap. Add the small flower, wrap stems to the end.

Wind Flower

Instructions for the Blue Wind Flower pictured above are on page 6.

ILLUSTRATIONS ARE SHOWN ACTUAL SIZE - REFER TO THE BASIC TECHNIQUES ON PAGE 2.

Bearded Iris

Irises convey a message of hope or sorrow.

Blue Bearded Iris

Instructions for small Yellow flowers on page 27.

Materials:
White-lined crystal, Orchid-lined crystal, or Dark Blue crystal, Blue crystal, White crystal, Green crystal and Yellow opaque seed beads; 28 gauge wire; wire cutters; floral tape; floral wire.

Stamen
Make 1 for each flower. Use the Orchid, White or Yellow beads to make a 1" **Single Loop**. Twist the loop twice.

Petals
Make 6 for each flower. Use Orchid, White or Dark Blue, Blue and White beads to make a 2" **Center Bar** with 5 loops. The center bar is $3/4$" long. For the Blue/White iris, make 3 mixed and 3 solid Light Blue petals.

Beards
Make 3 for each flower. For the Dark Blue/Blue flower, bead the mixed color petals. Use the Orchid, White or Yellow beads to thread a $3/4$" long piece. Hook the top of the wire over the loop at the bottom of the **Center Bar**. Twist the other end around the petal stem.

Iris Leaves
Make 2 for each flower. Use the Green beads to make a $3 1/2$" **Center Bar** with 3 loops. The Center Bar is $2 1/2$" long.

Assembly:
Hold the bearded petals together around the stamen. Cup 2 of the petals up over the top of the stamen. Bend the other petal down a bit and cup it up some, too. Arrange the remaining 3 petals under the center petals. Bend the outer petals downward. Wrap the stems for 3", add a leaf. Wrap the stems for 1" more, add the second leaf. Wrap the stems to the end.

Double Petals Flower

See instructions for Double Petals Flower on page 21.

White   *Purple*

ILLUSTRATIONS ARE SHOWN ACTUAL SIZE - REFER TO THE BASIC TECHNIQUES ON PAGE 2.

Canna Bud

Cannas grow in many colors. Choose a color to complement your own arrangement.

← Brace

Materials:
Blue crystal and Green crystal seed beads; 28 gauge wire; wire cutters; floral tape; floral wire.

Petals and Leaves
Make 2 petals for each bud. Use Blue beads to make a $2^5/8$" **Center Bar** with 3 loops. The center bar is $2^1/4$" long. Twist 1 petal 5 times. Make 1 leaf for each bud. Use the Green beads to make a $3^1/2$" **Center Bar** with 4 loops. The center bar is 3" long.

← Brace

Canna Leaf
Make 2 for each stem. Use Green beads to make a 9" **Center Bar** with 5 loops. The center bar is $7^7/8$" long.

Orchid and White Bearded Iris instructions on page 12

Orchid & White Bearded Iris

Assembly:
Place the twisted petal against the top $1^1/2$" of a piece of floral wire. Place the flat petal at the bottom of the twisted one. Wrap the flat petal around the twisted one, covering the floral wire. Place the same size Green leaf just below the bottom of the wrapped petal. Wrap the leaf around the petals. Wrap the stems and floral wire for 10" on the longer wire. Wrap the stems and floral wire for $8^1/2$" on the shorter wire. Add the stem leaves at either side. Wrap stems and wires together to the end.

ILLUSTRATIONS ARE SHOWN ACTUAL SIZE - REFER TO THE BASIC TECHNIQUES ON PAGE 2.

Bachelor Button

Bachelor buttons are a wish for hope in solitude.

Materials:
Yellow opaque, Moss-lined, Teal-lined and Purple-lined crystal seed beads; 28 gauge wire; wire cutters; floral tape; floral wire; 9 plastic ³/₄" Green leaves.

Stamen
Make 1 for each flower. Use Yellow beads to make a ¹/₂" **Single Loop**. Twist the loop once.

Top Layer
Make 1 for each flower. Use Moss beads to make 6 continuous ³/₈" **Single Loops**. Make the diameter ³/₈".

Second Layer
Make 1 for each flower. Use Purple beads to make 12 continuous ³/₈" **Single Loops**. Make the diameter ³/₈".

Third Layer
Use Purple beads to make 18 continuous ³/₈" **Single Loops**. Make the diameter ¹/₂".

Fourth Layer
Make 1 for the large flower only. Use Teal beads to make 21 continuous ³/₈" **Single Loops**. Make the diameter ³/₄". Bend the petals downward.

Assembly:
Push the stem of each layer through the circles of the subsequent layers for both flowers. Tape all the stems together for ³/₄". Lay the flowers aside. Cut a 6" piece of wire for each leaf. Tape the wires for 1" - 2", add 2 leaves below the top leaf, wrap the stems for ¹/₂". Make 3 bunches of leaves. Add the Small flower below one leaf group. Tape the stems for 2" and add the large flower and the other 2 leaf groups. Complete taping the stems.

Purple Petals Flower
Instructions on page 21.

Forget-Me-Not

Materials:
Peach crystal, Violet crystal, Orange opaque, Turquoise opaque and Green opaque seed beads; Green bugle beads; 28 gauge wire; wire cutters; Brown floral tape; floral wire.

Stamen
Use Peach or Violet beads to make 3 continuous ¹/₄" **Single Loops**.

Bud Stem
Use Turquoise beads to make ³/₁₆" **Single Loops**. Bead the stems with the bugle beads.

Petals
Use Orange or Turquoise beads to make 5 continuous ³/₈" **Single Loops**.

Large Leaf
Use Green beads to make leaf following instructions on page 4.

Assembly: Assemble the flower layers, tape stems 1". Add flowers and bud stems as desired.

ILLUSTRATIONS ARE SHOWN ACTUAL SIZE - REFER TO THE BASIC TECHNIQUES ON PAGE 2.

Daffodil

Materials:
Black opaque, Yellow opaque or crystal, White-lined crystal, Green crystal and Orange crystal seed beads; 28 gauge wire; wire cutters; floral tape; floral wire.

Stamen
Make 1 for each flower. Use Black beads to make 2 continuous $1/4$" **Single Loops**. Thread 1" of Green beads on each end of the wire. Twist the wire ends.

Inner Petals
Use Yellow opaque or crystal beads to make 12 continuous $1^1/2$" **Single Loops**. Option: Use Orange beads at the top $3/8$" of each petal.

Outer Petals
Make 6 for each flower. Use Yellow opaque or crystal or White crystal beads to make a $1^1/2$" **Center Bar** with 4 loops. The center bar is $1/2$" long.

Assembly:
Pull the inner petals up and brace the petals together tightly $3/8$" from the top. Place the stamen down through the center of the cup. Push the top of the inner petals down a bit to shape the bottom of the cup. Bend the top of the petals above the bracing to the outside. Arrange the outer petals around the bottom of the cup. Bend the petals out flat then bend up the tips of these petals. Tape the stems for $3^1/2$" and add a leaf. Tape for 1" more, add the other leaf. Finish taping the stems.

Daffodil and Tulip Leaf
Make 2 for each Daffodil. Make 4 for each Tulip stem. Use Green beads to make a $4^1/4$" **Center Bar** with 2 loops. The center bar is $3^3/4$" long.

Tulip

Materials:
Yellow and White opaque and Green crystal seed beads; Green crystal size 8 seed beads; 28 gauge wire; wire cutters; floral tape; floral wire.

Petals
Make 5 for each flower. Use Yellow beads to make a $1^1/2$" **Center Bar** with 3 loops. The center bar is $3/4$" long. Use White beads for the upper $3/4$" of the outer loop.

Assembly:
Make 3 flowers for each stem. Arrange the petals side by side and brace them together $3/4$" from the top. Pull the stems together and twist them. Make a $1/2$" calyx with the Green seed beads. Bead the stems for $4^1/2$" - 5" with size 8 beads. Add the leaves around the stems and wrap all stems to the end.

ILLUSTRATIONS ARE SHOWN ACTUAL SIZE - REFER TO THE BASIC TECHNIQUES ON PAGE 2.

Top Layer
Make 1 for each flower and bud. Use Red beads to make 4 continuous 1" **Single Loops**.

Second Layer
Make 1 for each flower and bud. Use Red beads to make 5 continuous 1" **Single Loops**.

Third Layer
Make 1 for each flower and bud. Use Peach beads to make 7 continuous 1" **Single Loops**. Push down on the top of each loop.

Fourth Layer
Make 1 for each flower, only. Use Coral beads to make 11 continuous 1" **Double Loop** petals.

Bud Leaves
Make 1 for each bud. Use Green beads to make 3 continuous 1" **Single Loops**. Twist each loop 2 - 3 times.

Stem Leaves
Make 9 for each stem. Use Green beads to make a 3" **Center Bar** with 2 loops. The center bar is 2¹/₂" long.

Assembly:
Make 3 flowers and 3 buds for each stem. Push the stem of each layer through the circles of the subsequent layers for each flower. Tape all the stems together for 5" - 6". Arrange the leaves around the stems of the flowers and buds. Complete taping the stems.

Dahlia

Dahlias express the instability of perfect love.

Materials:
Peach-lined crystal, Red crystal, Iridescent Coral and Green crystal seed beads; 28 gauge wire; wire cutters; floral tape; floral wire.

Stamen

Use Peach beads to make a ³/₈" x ³/₈" **Center Bar** with 1 loop. The center bar is ¹/₄" long. Leave the wires 2" - 3" long. Twist the wires below the center of the piece.

ILLUSTRATIONS ARE SHOWN ACTUAL SIZE - REFER TO THE BASIC TECHNIQUES ON PAGE 2.

Materials:
Blue crystal, Green-lined crystal and Dark Blue crystal seed beads; Green bugle beads 28 gauge wire; wire cutters; floral tape; floral wire.

Top Flowers
Make 4 for each stem. Make 2 stems.

Top Layer
Make 4 continuous 1/4" **Single Loops**. Use Blue beads for 2. Use Dark Blue beads for 2.

Bottom Layer
Make 4 continuous 3/8" **Single Loops**. Use Blue beads for 2. Use Dark Blue beads for 2.

Middle Flowers
Make 8 for each stem. Make 2 stems.

Top Layer
Make 4 continuous 3/8" **Single Loops**. Use Blue beads for 4. Use Dark Blue beads for 4.

Second Layer
Make 4 continuous 1/2" **Single Loops**. Use Blue beads for 4. Use Dark Blue beads for 4.

Bottom Flowers
Make 5 for each stem. Make 2 stems.

Top Layer
Make 4 continuous 3/8" **Single Loops**. Use Blue beads for 5. Use Dark Blue beads for 5.

Second Layer
Make 4 continuous 1" **Single Loops**. Use Blue beads for 5. Use Dark Blue beads for 5.

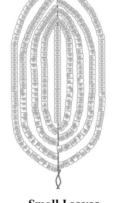

Small Leaves
Make 4 for each stem. Use Green beads to make a 2" **Center Bar** with 4 loops. The center bar is 1" long.

Large Leaf
Make 1 for each stem. Use Green seed and bugle beads to make a 4" **Center Bar** with 4 loops. The center bar is 3 1/4" long. Wrap the stem with Green seed beads for 2 1/4", as for a calyx.

Hyacinth

A hyacinth represents the playfulness of young love.

Assembly:
1. Make 2 stems for each arrangement. Push the stem of each layer through the circles of the subsequent layer for each flower. For the Top Flowers, tape each flower stem for 3" - 3 1/2". For the Middle Flowers, tape each flower stem for 2 3/4". Hold the stems of the Top and Middle Flowers together and tape them for 1". Arrange the Bottom Flowers around the stems of the upper flowers and wrap all the stems. Complete taping the stems to the desired length. Make the top stem 4" taller that the bottom one.

2. Tape the stem of the top and bottom small leaves for 2". Tape the stem of 1 of the other small leaves for 1/2". Tape the stems of the other small leaf for 1 1/4". Add the last 2 leaves 2" below the top one. Wrap all the stems for 1 1/2". Add the bottom leaf. Tape all the stems for 1 1/2".

3. Hold the stems of the flower stems, the small leaves and the large leaf together. Complete taping the stems.

ILLUSTRATIONS ARE SHOWN ACTUAL SIZE - REFER TO THE BASIC TECHNIQUES ON PAGE 2.

Sunflower

Sunflowers offer promises of power.

Materials:
Yellow and Orange opaque and Green and Dark Green crystal seed beads; Green size 8 seed beads; 28 gauge wire; wire cutters; floral tape; floral wire.

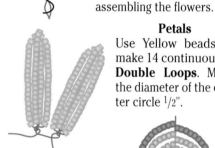

Center Stamen
Use Orange beads to make a 1" **Center Bar** with 5 loops. The center bar is 1/4" long. Leave the center wire long at the top and use it to wrap over the sides of the petal circle and then around itself when assembling the flowers.

Petals
Use Yellow beads to make 14 continuous 1" **Double Loops**. Make the diameter of the center circle 1/2".

Sunflower Leaves
Make 5 for each stem. Use Green and Dark Green beads to make a 4 1/2" **Center Bar** with 4 loops. The center bar is 3 1/2" long. Brace each leaf across the center.

Assembly:
Make 6 flowers for each stem. Make a 1" calyx for each flower with the small Green beads. Bead each stem with the size 8 Green beads for 5" or 6". Arrange the leaves around the flower stems. Wrap all the stems together.

Br ◄

Gerbera Daisy

Materials:
Yellow and White opaque and Green crystal seed beads; Green size 8 seed beads; 28 gauge wire; wire cutters; floral tape; floral wire.

Brace ►

Stamen
Use Yellow beads to make a 7/8" **Center Bar** with 5 loops. The center bar is 1/8" long. Leave the center wire long at the top and use it to wrap over the sides of the petal circle and then around itself when assembling the flowers.

Gerbera Leaves
Make 2 for each stem. Use Green beads to make a 5 1/4" **Center Bar** with 2 loops. The center bar is 4 3/4" long. Brace each leaf across the center.

Petals
Use White beads to make 15 continuous 7/8" **Double Loops**.

Assembly:
Make 3 flowers for each stem. Make a 1/2" calyx for each flower with the small Green beads. Bead each stem with the size 8 Green beads for 6 1/2". Arrange the leaves around the flower stems. Wrap all the stems together.

ILLUSTRATIONS ARE SHOWN ACTUAL SIZE - REFER TO THE BASIC TECHNIQUES ON PAGE 2.

Pot of Gold Allysum

Materials:
Yellow-lined crystal, Yellow opaque, Pink-lined crystal and Green crystal seed beads; 28 gauge wire; wire cutters; floral tape.

Yellow Flowers

Top Layer
Use any color of beads to make 4 continuous 3/8" petals with 2 graduating **Single Loops**.

Bottom Layer
Use any color of beads to make 5 continuous 1/2" petals with 2 graduating **Single Loops**.

Green Leaves

Leaf Layer
Make 1 for each flower. Use Green beads to make 5 continuous 3/8" **Single Loops**.

Filler Leaves
Make as many as needed for your arrangement. Use Green beads to make a 3/4" **Center Bar** with 2 loops. The center bar is 3/8" long.

Assembly:
Push the stem of each layer through the circles of the subsequent layer of petals and leaves for each flower. Wrap the stems together. Wrap the stem of each Filler Leaf.

Phlox

Materials:
Light Pink crystal, Rose crystal, White opaque and Green crystal seed beads; 28 gauge wire; wire cutters; floral tape. Optional: 3mm White pearls.

Stamen
Use any color of beads to make 3 continuous 3/16" **Single Loops**. Optional: Pearls may be used.

Large Flower Petals
Use any color of beads to make 4 continuous 1/2" petals with 2 graduating **Single Loops**.

Small Flower Petals
Use any color of beads to make 5 continuous 3/8" **Single Loops**.

Flower Leaves
Make 1 for small flowers, 2 for large flowers. Use Green beads to make 3/8" **Single Loops**. Thread 2 Green beads onto the stem below the leaf.

Assembly:
Push the stem of each layer through the circles of the subsequent layer. Wrap the stems together. Wrap the stems with 1 or 2 leaves.

ILLUSTRATIONS ARE SHOWN ACTUAL SIZE - REFER TO THE BASIC TECHNIQUES ON PAGE 2.

Pansy

Send pansies to let a lover know your thoughts of love before you state them.

Materials:
Orange crystal, Iridescent Purple, Silver-lined crystal and Iridescent Gunmetal seed beads; 28 gauge wire; wire cutters; floral tape; floral wire.

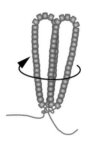

Buds
Use the Purple beads to make 2 continuous 1" **Single Loops**. Twist the loops together 3 times.

Bud Leaves
Make 2 for each bud. Use the Silver beads to make a continuous 5/8" **Single Loops**. Twist the loops together.

Leaf
Make 1 for each flower. Use Gunmetal beads to make a 1" **Center Bar** with 3 loops. The center bar is 1/4" long.

Stamen
Use Orange beads to make 2 continuous 1/4" **Single Loops**.

Side Petals
Make 2 for each flower. Use Purple and Silver beads to make a 1" **Center Bar** with 4 1/2 loops. The center bar is 1/4" long.

Bottom Petals
Make 2 for each flower. Use Purple and Silver beads to make a 3/4" petal with 4 graduating **Single Loops**.

Back Petal
Make 1 for each flower. Use Purple and Silver beads to make a 1 1/4" **Center Bar** with 5 1/2 loops. The center bar is 1/4" long.

Assembly:
Hold the Bottom Petals below the stamen. Place a Side Petal at either side of the stamen. Place the Back Petal above the stamen. Floral tape all the stems together for 1". Add the leaf and wrap all the stems together. Wrap bud stem. Wrap leaf stems together. Twist bud and leaf stems together.

ILLUSTRATIONS ARE SHOWN ACTUAL SIZE - REFER TO THE BASIC TECHNIQUES ON PAGE 2.

Double Petals Flower

Pictured in bouquets - White on page 12 - Purple on page 14.

Materials:
Yellow crystal and Purple or White crystal, Green crystal seed beads; 28 gauge wire; wire cutters; floral tape; floral wire.

Leaf
Make 5 for each flower. Use Green beads to make 1" **Center Bars** with 2 loops. The center bar is $1/2$" long.

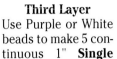

Top Layer
Use Yellow beads to make 9 continuous $3/4$" **Single Loops**.

Third Layer
Use Purple or White beads to make 5 continuous 1" **Single Loops**.

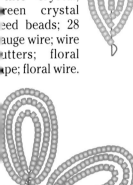

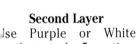

Second Layer
Use Purple or White beads to make 5 continuous 1" petals with 3 graduating **Single Loops**.

Bottom Layer
Make 5 for each flower. Use Purple or White beads to make $1 1/2$" **Center Bars** with 3 loops. The center bar is $1/2$" long.

Assembly:
Push the stem of each layer through the circles of the subsequent layers for each flower. Tape all the stems together for 2". Lay the flowers aside. Make a stem with 3 leaves, tape wires for 1". Tape the flower and leaf stems for $1 1/2$". Make a 1" stem with 2 leaves. Add these leaves, complete taping the stems.

Daisy

Daisies relate to innocence.

Materials:
Yellow opaque, White opaque and Green crystal seed beads; size 8 Green crystal seed beads; 28 gauge wire; wire cutters; floral tape; floral wire.

Stamen
Use Yellow beads to make a $1/4$" x $1/4$" **Center Bar** with 1 loop. The center bar is $1/8$" long. Leave the wires 2" - 3" long.

Petals
Use White beads to make 7 continuous $7/8$" **Center Bars** with 1 loop. the center bar is $7/8$" long.

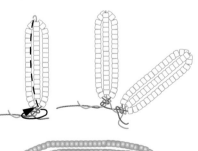

Leaf
Make 4 per stem. Use Green seed beads to make a 2" **Center Bar** with 5 loops. The center bar is $7/8$" long. Make a $5/8$" calyx. Bead the stems for $1 3/4$" with size 8 beads.

Assembly:
Make 5 flowers for each stem. Bend the stamen wires over the sides of the Petal circle. Make a $3/4$" calyx. Bead the stems for $3 1/2$" with the size 8 beads. Wrap the flower and leaf stems together.

ILLUSTRATIONS ARE SHOWN ACTUAL SIZE - REFER TO THE BASIC TECHNIQUES ON PAGE 2.

Snapdragon

Snapdragons suggest, "Let us be impetuous!"

Materials:
Yellow opaque, Red opaque, White opaque and Green opaque seed beads; 28 gauge wire; wire cutters; floral tape; floral wire.

Stamen
Use Yellow beads to make continuous $1/8$" **Single Loops**.

Petals
Use Red beads to make 4 continuous $1/2$" **Single Loops**.

Buds
Use any mixture of Green, Red, White and Yellow beads to make 2 continuous $1/2$" **Single Loops**.

Leaves
Use Green beads to make continuous $3/8$" **Single Loops**

Assembly:
Place the petals behind the stamen and wrap the stems together for 1". Add the leaves and continue wrapping the stems. For bud stems place the buds 1" apart on a stem.

Dianthus

Materials:
Yellow opaque, White opaque, Red opaque and Green opaque seed beads; 28 gauge wire; wire cutters; floral tape.

Leaves
Use Green beads to make 4 continuous $1/2$" **Single Loops.**

Stamen
Use the Yellow beads to make 6 continuous $3/8$" stacked **Single Loops**. Thread 2 Red beads onto one wire before twisting wires.

Petals
Use White beads to make 10 continuous $5/8$" **Single Loops.**

Assembly:
Place the stamen stems into the petal circle. Add the leaves at the back. Wrap all the stems together.

Moss Rose

Materials:
Yellow opaque, White opaque and Green opaque seed beads; 28 gauge wire; wire cutters; floral tape.

Head Center
Use Yellow and White beads. Begin with a $1/4$" **Single Loop**. Begin the next Loop and wrap the wire around the top center of the first loop.

Head
Make 3 or 4 graduating **Single Loops**. Thread the wire end through the first bead of the first loop.

Leaves
Use Green beads to make 3 continuous $3/8$" **Single Loops**.

Assembly:
Place the leaves behind the head and wrap the stems together for $1 1/4$". Make 3 flowers for each stem. Wrap all the stems together and add leaves as desired.

ILLUSTRATIONS ARE SHOWN ACTUAL SIZE - REFER TO THE BASIC TECHNIQUES ON PAGE 2.

Aster

Materials:
Light Blue, Blue, Dark Blue, White and Green crystal seed beads; size 8 Green crystal seed beads; 28 gauge wire; wire cutters; floral tape; floral wire.

Top Layer
Use White beads to make 3 continuous 1" **Single Loops**.

Second Layer
Use Light Blue beads to make 5 continuous $7/8$" **Single Loops**.

Third & Fourth Layers
Use Blue beads to make 6 continuous $7/8$" **Single Loops** for each layer.

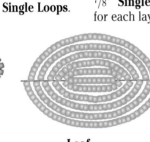

Bottom Layer
Use Dark Blue beads to make 8 continuous $7/8$" **Single Loops**.

Leaf
Make 3 for each leaf stem. Use Green beads to make $1 1/2$" **Center Bars** with 5 loops. The center bar is $1/2$" long.

Assembly:
Push the stems of each layer into the circle of each subsequent layer. Place the layers $1/4$" apart. Push all the petals upward. Make a 1" calyx with the smaller Green beads and bead the stem for 6" with the size 8 Green seed beads. Hold 3 leaves together, make a 1" calyx with the smaller Green beads and bead the stems for 5" with the size 8 Green seed beads.

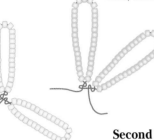

Quince

Materials:
Yellow opaque, Red opaque and Green opaque seed beads; 28 gauge wire; wire cutters; floral tape; floral wire.

Stamen
Use the Yellow beads to make 2 continuous $3/16$" **Single Loops**. Push the loops up together.

Petals
Use Red beads to make 4 continuous $3/8$" **Single Loops**.

Leaves
Use the Green beads to make 2 continuous $3/8$" **Single Loops**.

Buds
Use Red, Green and Yellow beads to make 2 continuous $3/8$" **Single Loops** with a $3/16$" Yellow loop in the center.

Assembly:
Place the petals behind the stamen and wrap the stems together for 1". Add the leaves and continue wrapping the stems. Repeat for the bud stems. Add bud stems to flower stems as desired.

ILLUSTRATIONS ARE SHOWN ACTUAL SIZE - REFER TO THE BASIC TECHNIQUES ON PAGE 2.

Pink Azalea

Materials:

Hot Pink crystal, Light Pink crystal, Pink crystal, Dark Pink crystal and Green crystal seed beads; 28 gauge wire; wire cutters; floral tape; floral wire.

Flower Stamen
Make 1 for each flower. Use Hot Pink beads to make a 3/8" **Center Bar** with 1 loop. The center bar is 1/4" long. Leave the wires 2" - 3" long.

Floweret Stamen
Make 1 for each flower. Use Hot Pink beads to make a 3/4" **Single Loop**. Twist the loop.

Stem Leaf
Make 9 for each stem. Use Green beads to make a 3" **Center Bar** with 2 loops. The center bar is 2 1/4" long.

Flower Top Layer
Make 1 for each flower. Use Light Pink beads to make 10 continuous 1" **Single Loops**.

Floweret Top Layer
Make 1 for each floweret. Use Light Pink beads to make 7 continuous 1" **Single Loops**.

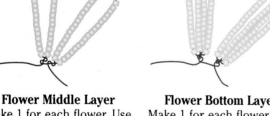

Flower Middle Layer
Make 1 for each flower. Use Dark Pink beads to make 9 continuous 1" **Single Loops**.

Flower Bottom Layer
Make 1 for each flower. Use Pink beads to make 11 continuous 1" **Double Loops**.

Floweret Middle Layer
Make 1 for each floweret. Use Dark Pink beads to make 7 continuous 1" **Single Loops**.

Floweret Leaves
Make 1 for each floweret. Use Green beads to make 3 continuous 1" **Single Loops**. Twist the loops

Assembly:

1. Make 3 flowers and 3 flowerets for each stem.
2. For the flowers, push the stem of each layer through the circles of the subsequent layer. Wrap the stems together for 5 1/2".
3. For the flowerets, wrap the wires of the stamen over the sides of the circle of the First Layer petals. Twist the stamen wires together. Push the stem of each layer through the circles of the subsequent layer. Add the leaves below the Middle Layer petals. Wrap the stems together for 5 1/2".
4. Arrange the stem leaves around the flower and floweret stems. Wrap all the stems together.

ILLUSTRATIONS ARE SHOWN ACTUAL SIZE - REFER TO THE BASIC TECHNIQUES ON PAGE 2.

Blue Azalea

Materials:
Dark Turquoise crystal, White crystal (flower and floweret Top Layers), Clear crystal flower and floweret Middle Layers), Blue iridescent (flower Bottom Layers) and Green crystal seed beads; 28 gauge wire; wire cutters; floral tape; floral wire.

Flower and Floweret Stamens
Make 1 for each flower and floweret. Use Dark Turquoise beads to make 3 continuous 1" **Single Loops**.

Follow the instructions for the Pink Azalea on page 24 to make and assemble the Blue Azalea stems, with the exception of the new stamen, above, for both flowers and flowerets.

Painted Daisy

Materials:
Light Blue opaque, Yellow opaque and Green crystal seed beads; size 8 Green crystal seed beads; 28 gauge wire; wire cutters; floral tape; floral wire.

Stamen
Use the Yellow beads to make a $3/8$" **Center Bar** with 1 loop. The center bar is $1/4$" long. Leave the wires 2" - 3" long.

Petals
Use Blue beads to make 10 continuous $5/8$" **Single Loops**.

Leaf
Make 2 for each stem. Use Green beads to make a $23/4$" **Center Bar** with 1 loop. The center bar is $23/4$" long.

Assembly:
Make 5 flowers for each stem. Wrap stamen wires over the petal circles. Bead each stem with the size 8 Green beads for $21/2$" - 5". Arrange the leaves around the flower stems. Wrap all the stems together.

Snowbell

Materials:
Blue, Yellow, White and Green opaque crystal seed beads; 28 gauge wire; wire cutters; floral tape; floral wire.

Stamen
Use White and Yellow beads to make 3 continuous $1/8$" **Single Loops**. Add $1/4$" of White beads to the stem.

Petals
Use Blue beads to make 5 continuous $5/8$" **Single Loops**.

Leaves
Make 1 for each flower stem. Use Green beads to make a $5/8$" **Single Loop**.

Assembly:
Brace the petals together $1/4$" from the top. Insert the stamen and wrap the stems for 2". Add a leaf, wrap for 1". Repeat with 2 more flowers and leaves. Hold the 3 flowers together to wrap them.

Bell Flower

Materials:
White opaque and Green opaque seed beads; 28 gauge wire; wire cutters; floral tape; floral wire; purchased Black stamens.

Petals
Make 3. Use White to make a 1" petal with 3 graduating **Single Loops**. At the end of the first loop, run the wires through 2 other beads, as shown.

Leaf
Use Green beads to make a $21/2$" **Single Loop**.

Brace

Petals
On the second loop, use the top bead of the first loop to anchor the top.

Assembly:
Brace petals together. Insert the stamens into the flower and wrap stems as desired. Add 2 leaves to stem, wrap to the end.

ILLUSTRATIONS ARE SHOWN ACTUAL SIZE - REFER TO THE BASIC TECHNIQUES ON PAGE 2.

White Flowers

Materials:
Yellow opaque, White opaque and Green crystal seed beads; 28 gauge wire; wire cutters; floral tape.

Stamen
Use the Yellow beads to make a 1" **Single Loop**. Twist the loop at the bottom.

Petals
Make 6 for each flower. Use White beads to make a $1^{1}/2$" **Center Bar** with 5 loops. The center bar is $^{1}/2$" long.

Veins
For 3 of the petals, use Yellow beads to thread a $^{1}/2$" long piece. Hook the top of the wire over the loop at the bottom of the **Center Bar**. Twist the ends around the petal stem.

Leaf
Make 2 for each flower. Use Green beads to make a $4^{1}/2$" **Center Bar** with 2 loops. The center bar is 4" long. Brace each leaf across the center.

Buds
Make 3 to 7 for each bud stem. Use White and Yellow beads to make 2 continuous $^{1}/4$" **Single Loops**.

Assembly:
Arrange 3 veined petals around the stamen. Place the other 3 petals behind and between the veined ones. Wrap the stems for 3". Add 2 leaves and continue wrapping the stems. For the bud stems, place the buds 1" apart on each stem.

 ← **Brace**

Primroses

Also pictured on page 22.

Materials:
White, Yellow and Green opaque seed beads; 28 gauge wire; wire cutters; floral tape; floral wire.

Petals

Make 3 for each stem. Use the White beads to make 5 continuous $^{5}/8$" **Single Loops**. Twist the wire ends once. Thread 2 Yellow beads onto one wire end. Bend the beaded wire across the center of the flower and over the circle to the back. Bend the unbeaded wire to the back. Twist the wires together below the center circle.

Buds
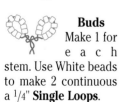
Make 1 for each stem. Use White beads to make 2 continuous a $^{1}/4$" **Single Loops**.

Leaf

Make 2 for each stem. Use Green beads to make a $^{3}/4$" **Single Loop**.

Assembly:
Wrap each flower and bud stem for 1". Add the leaves and wrap all the stems together for 2". Add another stem and wrap all the stems together.

ILLUSTRATIONS ARE SHOWN ACTUAL SIZE - REFER TO THE BASIC TECHNIQUES ON PAGE 2.

26 *Beaded Flowers and Garlands*

Pyrethrum

Materials:
White, Yellow, Red and Green opaque seed beads; 28 gauge wire; wire cutters; floral tape; floral wire.

Top Layer
Make 3 for each stem. Use the Yellow beads to make 6 continuous 3/8" **Double Loops**. Twist the wire ends once. Thread 2 Red beads onto one wire end. Bend the beaded wire across the center of the flower and over the circle to the back. Bend the unbeaded wire to the back. Twist the wires together below the center circle.

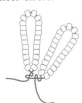

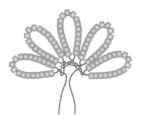

Bottom Layer
Use White beads to make 11 continuous 5/8" **Single Loops**.

Flower Leaves
Use Green beads to make 5 continuous 1/2" **Single Loops**.

Stem Leaves
Use Green beads to make 3 continuous 5/8" **Single Loops**.

Assembly:
Arrange the layers and wrap the stems of each flower for 2". Add the Stem Leaves and wrap all the stems together.

Golden Candles

Also pictured on page 12.

Materials:
Yellow opaque and Green crystal seed beads; 28 gauge wire; wire cutters; floral tape.

Flowers
Make a 1 1/2" **Single Loop**. Twist the top half once. Twist the bottom half once. Fold the top down and thread one of the bottom wires through the top loop. Twist the bottom wires together to form the stem. Twist the flower 4 times. Make 21.

Flower Leaves
Make 2 for each flower. Use Green beads to make a 1/2" **Single Loop**.

Stem Leaves
Make 4 for each group of flowers. Use Green beads to make a 2" **Center Bar** with 2 loops. The center bar is 1 1/2" long.

Assembly:
Wrap the stems of each flower and 2 flower leaves for 2". Repeat for each flower. Hold all the stems together and arrange the stem leaves around them. Wrap all the stems together.

ILLUSTRATIONS ARE SHOWN ACTUAL SIZE - REFER TO THE BASIC TECHNIQUES ON PAGE 2.

Poinsettia Brooch

Looking for a great and unique holiday idea? Make a wreath of beaded Red and White poinsettias! Ooh-la-la!

Materials:
Dark Red crystal and Dark Green crystal seed beads; 3 Black 6mm pearls; 28 gauge wire; wire cutters; floral tape; $1^1/4$" pin back.

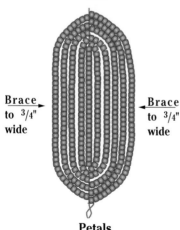

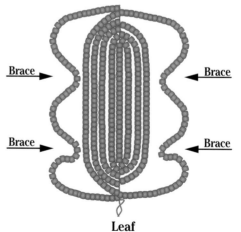

Brace to $3/4$" wide

Brace to $3/4$" wide

Brace → **Brace**

Brace → **Brace**

Assembly:
Arrange 3 petals around the stamens. Arrange the remaining petals behind and in between the first ones around the back of the flower. Place the leaf between 2 of the bottom petals. Floral tape all the stems together for $1^1/2$" adding the pin back on the last round of wraps.

Stamen
Make 3 for each flower. Use Red seed beads to make a $1/8$" **Single Loop**, thread on a Black bead. Twist the wires together.

Petals
Make 6 for each flower. Use Red beads to make a 2" **Center Bar** with $4^1/2$" loops. The center bar is $1^1/4$" long. Brace each petal across the center to be $3/4$" wide.

Leaf
Make 1 for each flower. Use Green beads to make a 2" **Center Bar** with $4^1/2$" loops, as shown. The Center Bar is $1^1/4$" long. Brace the leaf at each point indicated to secure the loops.

ILLUSTRATIONS ARE SHOWN ACTUAL SIZE - REFER TO THE BASIC TECHNIQUES ON PAGE 2.

Camellia Brooches

Camellias exemplify honest excellence.

Materials:
Red-lined crystal, Yellow crystal, Clear crystal, Pink-lined crystal, Blue-lined crystal, Grass Green crystal, Lime Green crystal and Green-lined crystal seed beads; 28 gauge wire; wire cutters; floral tape; floral wire; 1" pin back for each brooch; two $1/2$" Frosted, Gold, or Purple glass peaches for each brooch; 1 Green 1" glass leaf for each brooch.

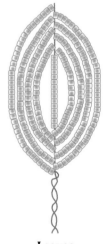

Center Level Petals
Make 5 for each flower. Use the Red, Yellow or Clear beads to make a $1/2$" petal with 2 graduating **Single Loops**. Wrap the wire of the second loop around the top of the first loop before finishing.

Second Level Petals
Make 5 for each flower. Use the Red, Yellow or Clear beads to make a $5/8$" petal with 3 graduating **Single Loops**. Wrap the wire of each loop around the top of the previous loop before finishing.

Third Level Petals
Make 8 for each flower. Use the Red, Yellow or Clear beads to make a $3/4$" petal with 4 graduating **Single Loops**. Wrap the wire of each loop around the top of the previous loop before finishing.

Fourth Level Petals
Make 7 for each flower. Use the Pink, Grass or Blue beads to make a $3/4$" petal with 4 graduating **Single Loops**. Wrap the wire of each loop around the top of the previous loop before finishing.

Leaves
Make 3 for each flower. Use the Green-lined or Lime beads to make a $1 3/4$" **Center Bar** with $3 1/2$ loops. The center bar is $3/4$" long.

Assembly:
1. Arrange the Center Petals. Place the Second Level Petals under the center ones, bending the petals down slightly. Place the Third Level Petals at the back, overlapping the petals slightly. Place the Fourth Level Petals at the back, overlapping them as necessary. Arrange the leaves around the back at the bottom of the flower. Wrap wire around all the stems.

2. Floral tape each stem of each peach for $3/4$". Cut a 3" piece of floral wire for each glass leaf. Floral tape the stem for $1/2$". Floral tape the peach and leaf stems together.
3. Wrap the stems of the beaded leaves individually. Add the flower stems and floral tape all the stems together for $1 3/4$", attaching the pin back with the last wrap.

ILLUSTRATIONS ARE SHOWN ACTUAL SIZE - REFER TO THE BASIC TECHNIQUES ON PAGE 2.

Windflower Barrette

Also pictured on page 2 (Silver/Champagne) and on page 6 (Bronze/Black)

Materials:
Champagne crystal, Silver-lined crystal and Green iridescent seed beads; 2
gauge wire; wire cutters; 3 1/2" barrette; 4" of 1/2" White satin ribbon; 10" of 3/
Green velvet ribbon; E6000 adhesive.

Stamen
Make 1. Use Champagne beads to make 2 continuous 1/8" **Single Loops**. Twist the wires together.

Petals and Leaves
Use Silver beads to make a windflowe according to the instructions on pag 6. Use the Green beads to make leaves according to the instruction on page 6.

Assembly:

 Barrette   Scrunch the leaf down

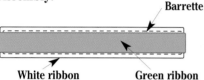

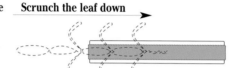

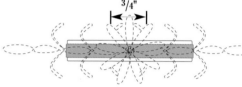

White ribbon   Green ribbon

1. Center and glue the White ribbon onto the barrette. Cut a 4" piece of Green ribbon. Glue in in place over the center of the White ribbon.

2. Cut the leaf stems to 3/4" long. Glue 1 leaf stem on the barrette with the end overlapping the center 3/8". Scrunch the leaf to be 1" longer than the piece. Repeat.

3. Cut the flower stem to 3/8" long. Bend th stem to one side. Place the flower at the cente of the barrette. Use the remaining Green ribbo to wrap around ends of stems and center c barrette. Glue the ribbon in place.

Impatiens
Hair Dangle

Materials:
Green crystal, Purple iridescent crystal and Toast iridescent crystal seed beads; 28 gauge Black wire; wire cutters; bobby pin.

Stamen
Make 1. Use Green and Purple beads to make a 1/2" petal with 2 graduating **Single Loops**.

Petals
Make 5. Use Purple beads to make 3/4" **Center Bars** with 1 loop. Twist the loop wire around the center wire. Clip the ends close. Twist the stems together. Cut the stems 1/2" long.

Spray
Make 1. Use Toast beads to make an arrangement of 1/4" **Single Loops**. Work each stem of each branch individually. Thread the beads, then twist the wires below them. Twist the wires of each branch last.

Assembly:
Place the flower on top of the twisted ends of the Spray, place the leaf at th back. Twist the Spray and Leaf stems together, wrap wire around the flowe stems, then wrap wire around the top of the pin.

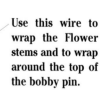

Use this wire to wrap the Flower stems and to wrap around the top of the bobby pin.

Leaf
Make 1. Use th Green beads t make a **loo tree** with 1/4 Single Loops.

ILLUSTRATIONS ARE SHOWN ACTUAL SIZE - REFER TO THE BASIC TECHNIQUES ON PAGE 2.

Pussy Willow Dangle

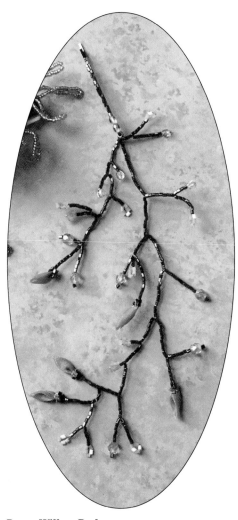

Begin here with 12" wire.

Begin 5" from the end of one 12" wire. Bend the wire and wrap the wire loop around open end of the bobby pin. Thread Brown beads, then 2 Pink 4mm beads on the 7" end of the wire. Wrap the 5" end of the wire around the beads and pin and around the top of the bobby pin. Wrap the long wire around the pin several times. Begin beading the branches.

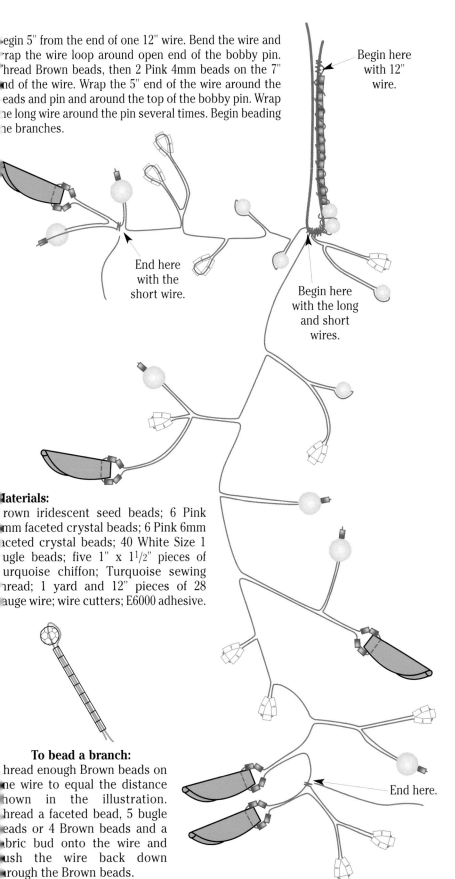

End here with the short wire.

Begin here with the long and short wires.

End here.

Materials:

Brown iridescent seed beads; 6 Pink 4mm faceted crystal beads; 6 Pink 6mm faceted crystal beads; 40 White Size 1 bugle beads; five 1" x 1¹/₂" pieces of Turquoise chiffon; Turquoise sewing thread; 1 yard and 12" pieces of 28 gauge wire; wire cutters; E6000 adhesive.

To bead a branch:

Thread enough Brown beads on the wire to equal the distance shown in the illustration. Thread a faceted bead, 5 bugle beads or 4 Brown beads and a fabric bud onto the wire and push the wire back down through the Brown beads.

Pussy Willow Buds
Use a 1" x 1¹/₂" piece of chiffon for each bud.

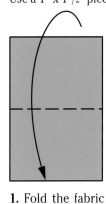

1. Fold the fabric in half to make a 1" x ³/₄" piece.

2. Fold over each corner to the center of the piece.

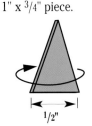

3. Roll the bud around itself so it is half as wide as it was before.

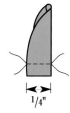

4. Gather stitch across the bottom, tucking the bud a bit. Secure threads.

ILLUSTRATIONS ARE SHOWN ACTUAL SIZE - REFER TO THE BASIC TECHNIQUES ON PAGE 2.

Basic Techniques for Garlands

Use garlands to decorate candles, lamps, picture frames, boxes or anything else that stands still!

1. Use 2 yards of wire. Cut the wire in half. Begi 2" from the ends of the wires. Twist the wire together for ¹/₂".

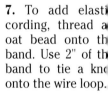

2. Wrap the ends of th wires around the twis 2 or 3 times to form ¹/₄" loop at the end.

3. Cut the wire end close to the twists.

4. Begin addin beads accordin to the illustratio for each garland

5. Twist the wire together afte each bead add tion as shown i the illustrations.

6. End the wires according to Steps 1 - 3, above.

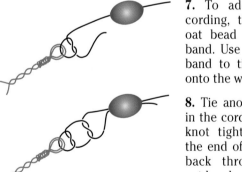

7. To add elasti cording, thread a oat bead onto th band. Use 2" of th band to tie a kn onto the wire loop.

8. Tie another kn in the cord. Pull th knot tight. Threa the end of the cor back through th oat bead.

9. Glue the knots. Pus the bead down to th knots. Trim the end of th cord. Measure the co around your head for and cut it as neede Repeat Steps 7 - 9 at th other end of the garland

Bead Flowers

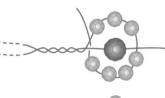

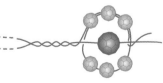

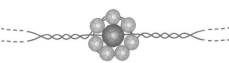

1. Thread one wire through the center bead. Thread the other wire through the top beads, over the center wire and then through the bottom beads. Go under the center wire.

2. Thread through the top beads again. Wrap the wire around the center wire.

3. Twist the wire around the center wire after the flower as shown in the illustration. Continue beading the garland.

ILLUSTRATIONS ARE SHOWN ACTUAL SIZE - REFER TO THE BASIC TECHNIQUES ON PAGE 2.

Garlands

General Materials for each Garland:

Seed beads, faceted beads, oat beads, flower beads and leaf beads; 2 yards of Silver, Gold, Copper or Black 28 gauge wire; wire cutters; 12" of elastic cording; E6000 adhesive. **Optional:** Two 8mm jump rings; two 5" pieces of beaded necklace chain; necklace clasps.

Assembly:

Follow the Basic Techniques on page 32 to begin and end garlands. Repeat the pattern of the garland to the center. Work the other half in a mirror image of the first half. To make a necklace, attach a jump ring in the loop at each end of the garland and attach a piece of chain to each jump ring. Attach the clasps at each end of the chains.

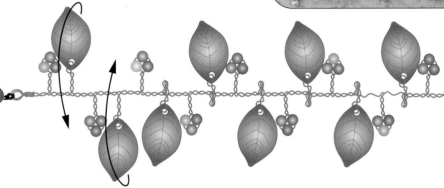

Materials: 66 assorted 3mm Green, Turquoise, Royal Blue and Purple pearl beads; 21 Green 15 x 21mm Dogwood leaves; 2 Dark Purple Pearl 9 x 6mm oat beads.

Materials: 31 White 4mm pearls; 6 Pink and 5 Violet 12mm Dogwood flowers; 10 each Rose and Violet 6mm Baby's breath flowers; 11 Green 15 x 10mm Dogwood leaves; 2 Dark Pink 9 x 6mm oat beads.

Materials: 31 White 4mm pearls; 6 Yellow and 5 Pink 12mm Dogwood flowers; 10 each Rose and Yellow 6mm Baby's breath flowers; 11 Green 15 x 10mm Dogwood leaves; 2 Yellow Pearl 9 x 6mm oat beads.

Materials: 80 Moss Green 4mm pearls; 8 Gold 6mm pearls; 24 each White and Dark Pink and 6mm pearls; 2 Moss Green 9 x 6mm oat beads.

Materials: 9 Petal Pink 18mm Star Flowers, 16 Peach Pearl 12mm Dogwood flowers; 25 Peach 4mm pearls; 9 Green 15 x 10mm Dogwood leaves; 2 Peach 9 x 6mm oat beads.

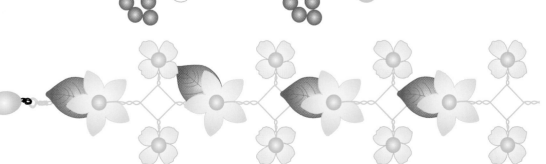

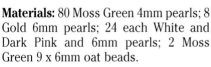

ILLUSTRATIONS ARE SHOWN ACTUAL SIZE - REFER TO THE BASIC TECHNIQUES ON PAGE 2.

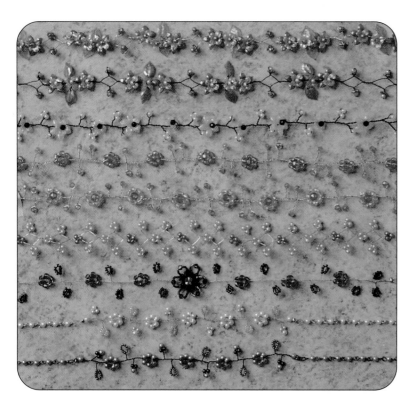

Garlands

Use garlands to decorate candles, lamps, picture frames, boxes or anything else that stands still!

General Materials:
Seed beads, faceted beads, oat beads flower beads and leaf beads; 2 yards of Silver, Gold, Copper or Black 2 gauge wire; wire cutters; 12" of elastic cording; E600 adhesive. **Optional:** Two 8mm jump rings; two pieces of beaded necklace chain; necklace clasps.

Assembly:
Follow the Basic Techniques on page 32 to begin and end garlands. Repeat the pattern of the garland to the center. Work the other half in a mirror image of the first half. To make a necklace, attach a jump ring in the loop at each end of the garland and attach a piece of chain to each jump ring. Attach the clasps at each end of the chains.

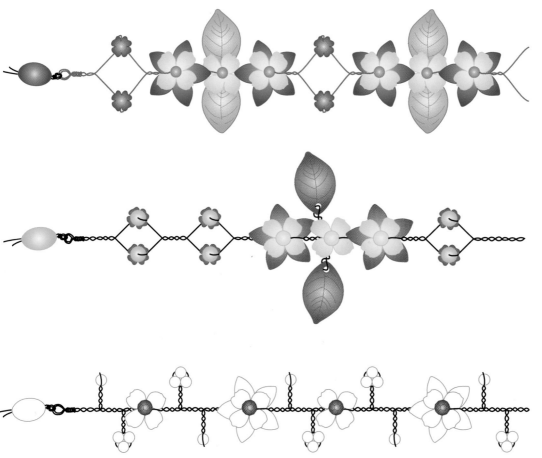

Materials: 32 Turquoise 3mm pearls; 18 Pink 12mm Dogwood Flower beads; 12 Violet 18mm Star Flower beads; 12 Mint 15 x 10mm Dogwood leaves; 2 Violet 9 x 6mm oat beads.

Materials: 14 Green 6mm Baby's breath flower beads; 8 Green 18mm Star Flower beads; 12 Pink 12mm Dogwood Flower beads; 12 Pink and 12 Yellow 4mm pearls; 14 Violet 6mm Baby's breath flower beads; 8 Green 15 x 10mm Dogwood leaf beads; 2 Pink 9 x 6mm oat beads.

Materials: 11 Black opaque 4mm faceted beads; 44 White 4mm pearls; 5 White Pearl 18mm Star Flower beads; 11 White Pearl 12mm Dogwood Flower beads; White Pearl 9 x 6mm oat beads.

ILLUSTRATIONS ARE SHOWN ACTUAL SIZE - REFER TO THE BASIC TECHNIQUES ON PAGE 2.